Other Works by Susan Striker Published by Henry Holt

The Anti-Coloring Book® *(with Edward Kimmel)*

The Second Anti-Coloring Book® *(with Edward Kimmel)*

The Third Anti-Coloring Book®

The Fourth Anti-Coloring Book®

The Fifth Anti-Coloring Book®

The Sixth Anti-Coloring Book®

The Anti-Coloring Book® of Exploring Space on Earth

The Anti-Coloring Book® of Masterpieces

The Inventor's Anti-Coloring Book®

The Mystery Anti-Coloring Book®

The Newspaper Anti-Coloring Book®

The Circus Anti-Coloring Book® *(with Jason Striker)*

The Anti-Coloring Book® of Celebrations

Artists at Work

A Literature-Based Anti-Coloring Book®
on Careers in Art

For Those Who Are Young at Art®

Susan Striker

Illustrations by Sally Schaedler

An Owl Book
Henry Holt and Company
New York

Dedicated with gratitude to
Greg Hamlin
who has been such a great supporter of these books;
and in memory of
Herberta W. Sinkus
who believed early in my teaching talents;
and my mother,
Sylvia Glaser
who insisted that if I majored in art
I had to get a teaching degree as well!
With sincere thanks to
Debbie and Jennie of Mr. McGregor's Garden Bookstore in Ft. Wayne, Indiana;
Ken Eckert of Barnes and Noble Jr., East Eighty-sixth Street, New York City;
Betty MacLeod, The Tattered Cover, Denver, Colorado;
the great media specialists of the Glenville, New Lebanon, and North Street Schools;
The Byram Schubert Library and Noreen Rogers, reading consultant,
for keeping me supplied with wonderful children's books;
and Le Ann Hinckle for keeping it all together for me.

Henry Holt and Company, Inc.
Publishers since 1866
115 West 18th Street
New York, New York 10011

Henry Holt ® is a registered
trademark of Henry Holt and Company, Inc.

Published in Canada by Fitzhenry & Whiteside Ltd.,
195 Allstate Parkway, Markham, Ontario L3R 4T8.

ISBN 0-8050-3413-7

Henry Holt books are available for special
promotions and premiums. For details
contact: Director, Special Markets.

First Edition—1997

Printed in the United States of America
All first editions are printed on acid-free paper∞

1 3 5 7 9 10 8 6 4 2

Introduction

As I drove home from work one evening, I listened to a radio talk show hosted by an expert in finance. A teenager who wanted to be an artist when she finished school telephoned and asked about potential earnings. The expert advised her **not** to be an artist because so few earn decent incomes. At that time I was earning the highest salary I had ever earned in my life, as an arts administrator. I spent a lot of my time counseling teenagers to pursue careers in the arts and was disappointed by the misinformed advice given to the caller. The conversation inspired me to write this book.

Recently I was reminded of that incident when I overheard a fifth grade boy talking to his friends during an art class. "The only time I'm ever happy in school is once a week when we come to art." I suggested to the young man that he consider a career in art so he could *always* be happy. He looked at me as if I was a raving maniac, and assured me that a career in art was not something he could realistically consider. As young as he was, he had already bought into the notion that artists tend to be poor. The image of a starving artist in a garret on the Left Bank of Paris, who paints pictures that won't be appreciated until long after his death, permeates the public's idea about careers in art. However, there are many men and women who draw, paint, and design for a living and earn handsome and secure paychecks. As in most every field, there is potential for greatness and wealth.

Work is one of the noblest expressions of the human spirit. From childhood through old age, while making art we learn the joy of working to the best of our abilities. Art can be the visible evidence of work performed at the highest possible level as well as a means of self-expression and communication. While creating, artists engage problem solving and critical thinking skills. These skills are at the very heart of education. Students should be encouraged to create as well as describe, analyze, and interpret visual images in order to express themselves thoughtfully. Since the stone age, people have created art that has offered future generations of researchers invaluable information about humanity. If the prevailing prejudice against the arts continues, we will become a civilization known in history for not truly valuing art. Bob Herbert of the *New York Times* reported that out of two hundred high schools in New York City, less than a dozen have viable art programs. "The sad fate of many youngsters is to travel the bumpy road of the public school system without ever discovering they have artistic talent. Others may recognize they have talent but never learn of the career opportunities that would be available if they were properly trained."

Pride in workmanship can be its own reward, but society also rewards artists monetarily. This book will expose children to a full range of careers in the arts, which may lead to successful and rewarding careers later in their lives. *Artists at Work* also includes a listing of children's books that corresponds with each career presented. For more detailed information about the diverse professions in the arts I also recommend *Careers in Art* by Gerald F. Brommer and Joseph A. Gatto (Davis Publications, 1984), which features a comprehensive list of careers in the arts with detailed descriptions of what each profession entails. It also includes a listing of specialized schools and an extensive bibliography. *How to Survive and Prosper as an Artist* by Caroll Michells (Henry Holt, 1992) addresses the often forgotten issues of marketing and public relations for artists.

"LOOK, SON, WE KNOW YOU'VE HAD YOUR HEART SET ON BECOMING A DOCTOR, BUT WOULD YOU AT LEAST THINK ABOUT GOING TO ART SCHOOL?!"

Courtesy of Gary Brookins

"Art's a staple. Like bread or wine or a warm coat in winter. Those who think it is a luxury have only a fragment of a mind. Man's spirit grows hungry for art in the same way his stomach growls for food."   —Irving Stone

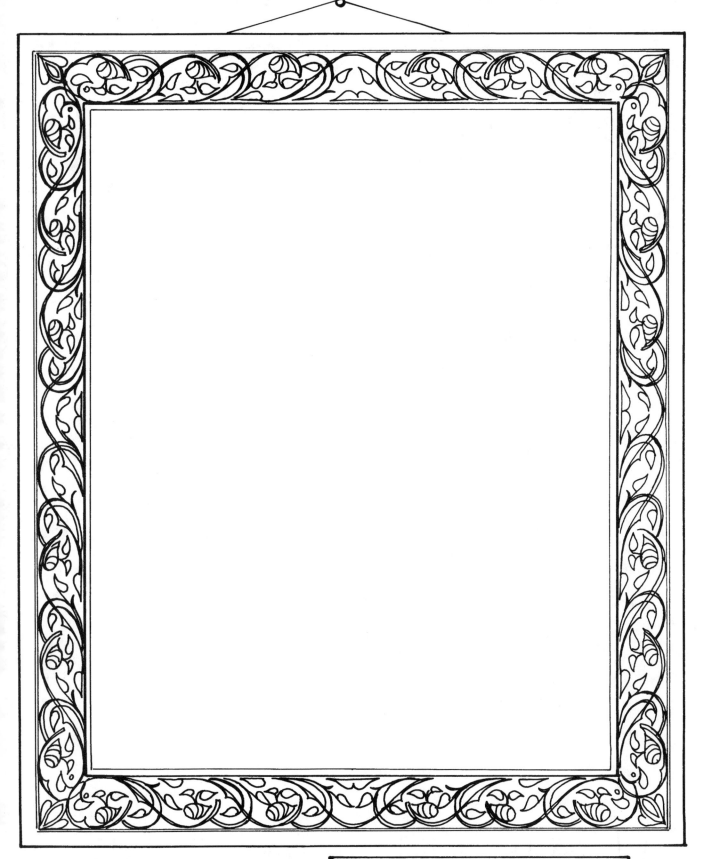

ABSTRACT PAINTER

Abstract artists paint with the colors and in the shapes of their dreams. Their works hang on walls in museums, offices, and homes for everyone to enjoy.

GOOD BOOKS

The Newspaper
Gail Gibbons

Paperboy
Mary Kay Kroeger
and Louise Borden
Illustrated by Ted Lewin

ADVERTISING ARTIST

Advertising artists create ads to help sell products.

Your ad is scheduled to appear in tomorrow's paper.

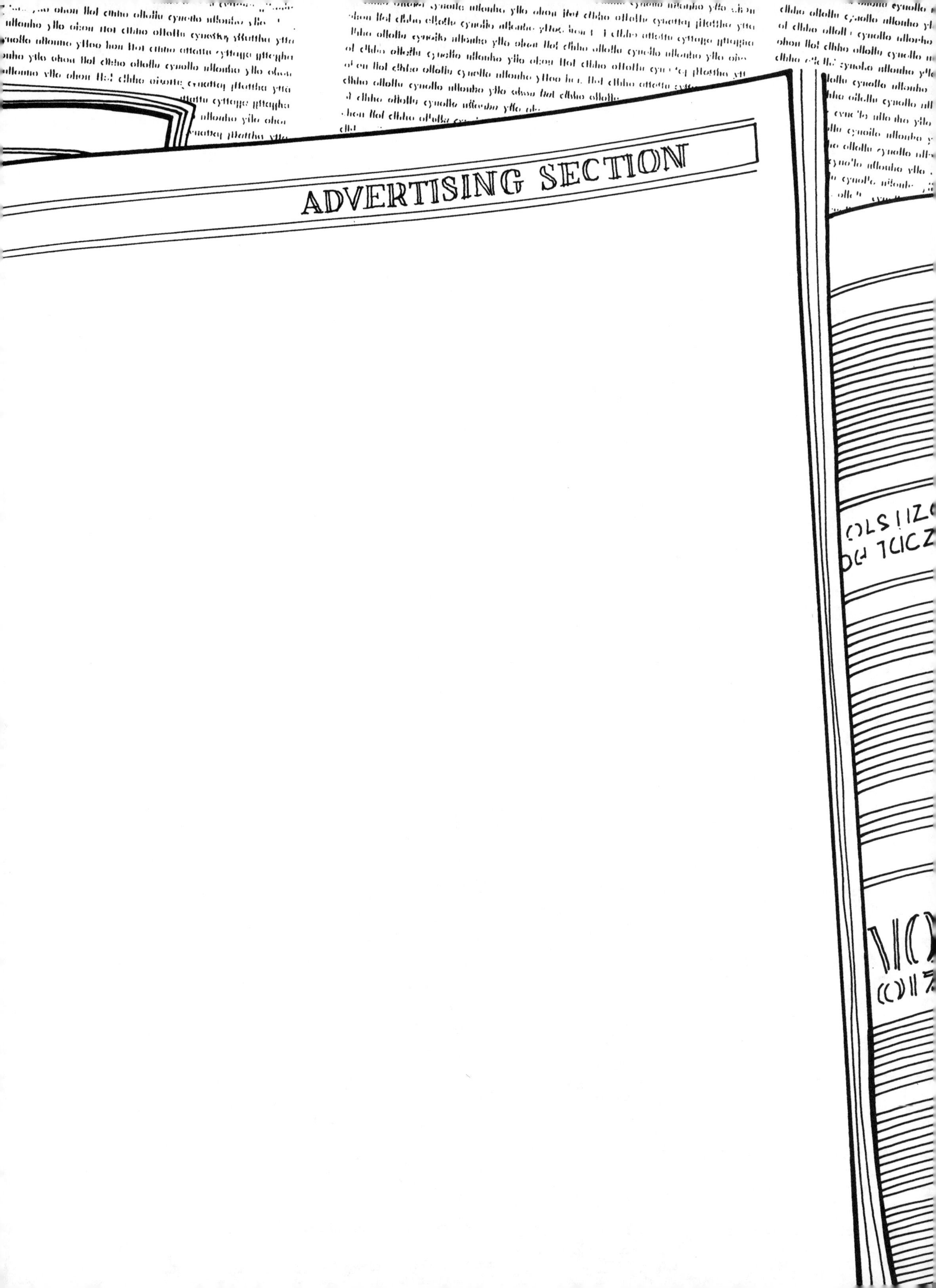
ADVERTISING SECTION

The Artist and the Architect, Demi

My House
Lisa Desimini

The House That Bob Built
Illustrated by
Robert A. M. Stern

A House Is a House for Me
Mary Ann Hoberman

What It Feels Like to Be a
Building, Forest Wilson

Frankie's Bau-Wau Haus
Melanie Brown and
Anthony Lawlor

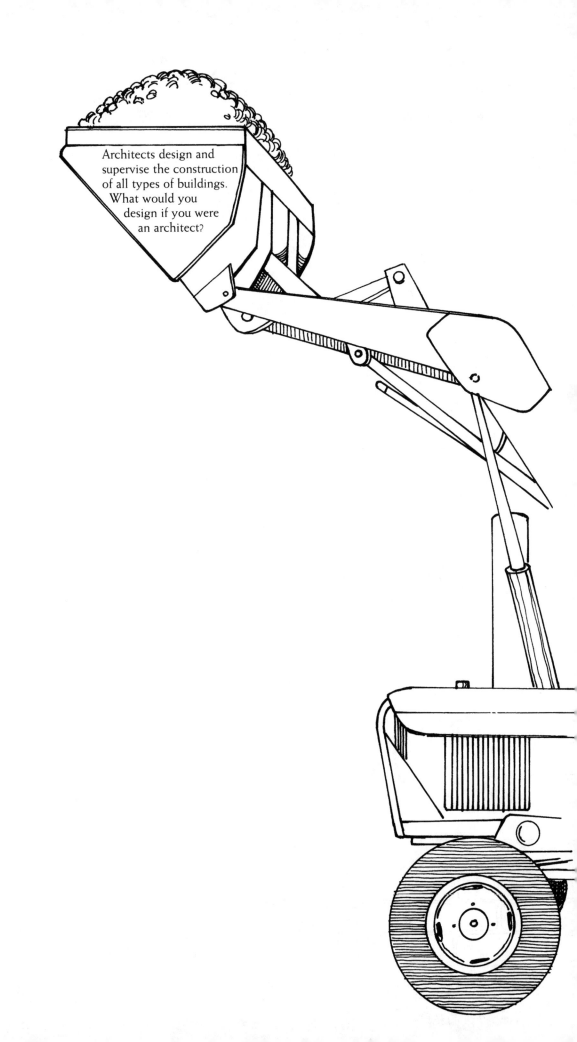

Architects design and
supervise the construction
of all types of buildings.
What would you
design if you were
an architect?

ART TEACHER

The Art Lesson
Tomie de Paola

Art teachers help other people express themselves through art. What kind of pictures are the students in this class painting?

The Goodbye Painting
Linda Berman
Illustrated by Mark Hannon

The Mud Family
Betsy James, Illustrated by Paul Morin

Art Therapists

Art therapists help people solve problems and face fears through their art. Patients can draw, paint, or make sculpture.

Spike
Katherine Potter

Artists design the covers of books to reflect content and attract potential buyers. The illustrator draws pictures inside the book that help the author tell the story.

BOOK ILLUSTRATOR

The Secret Art of Dr. Seuss, Introduction by Maurice Sendak

Color, Ruth Heller

From Pictures to Words: A Book About Making a Book
Janet Stevens

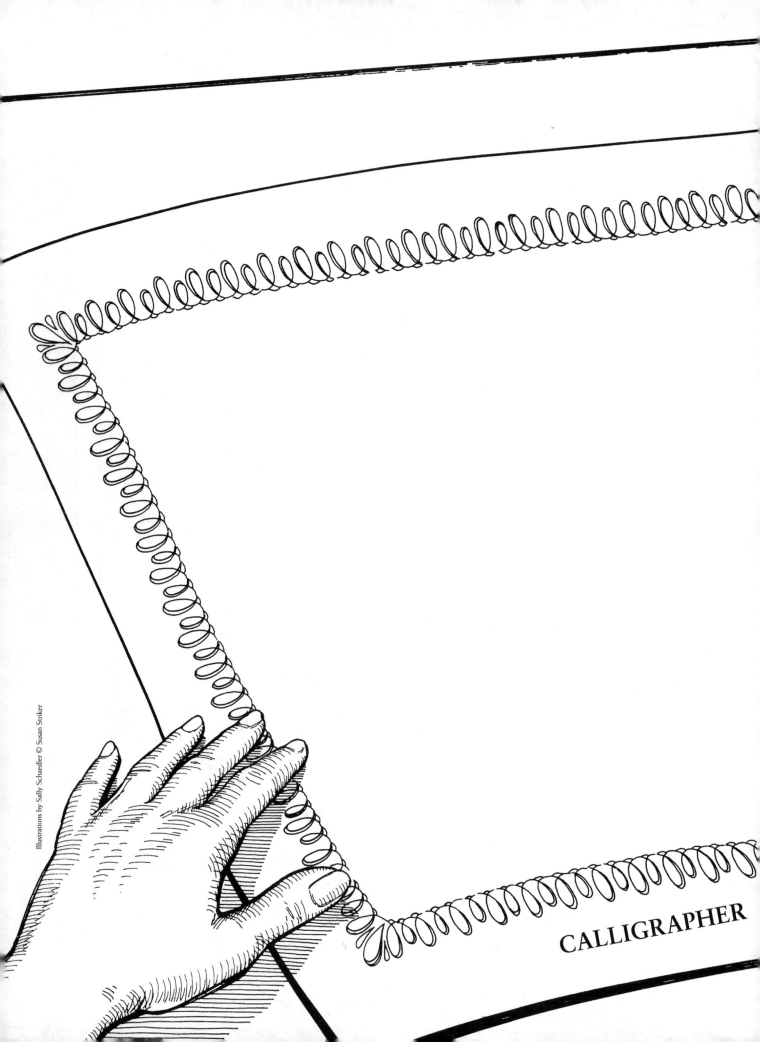

CALLIGRAPHER

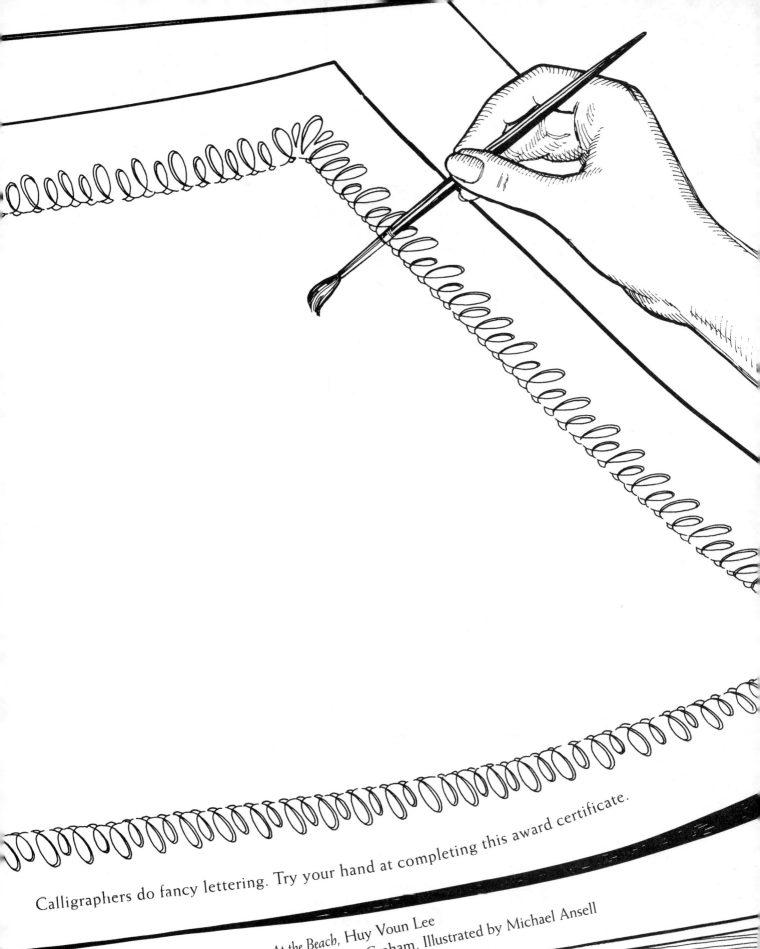

Calligraphers do fancy lettering. Try your hand at completing this award certificate.

At the Beach, Huy Voun Lee
Bird's Eye, Judy Graham, Illustrated by Michael Ansell

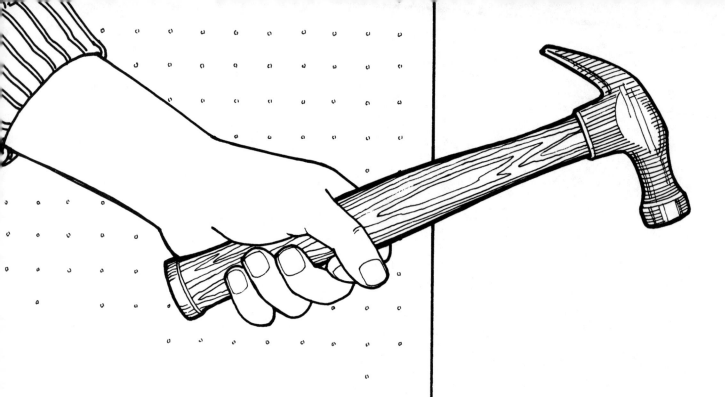

Illustrations by Sally Schaedler © Susan Striker

CARPENTER

Carpenters use wood, saws, screws, and nails for their creations.

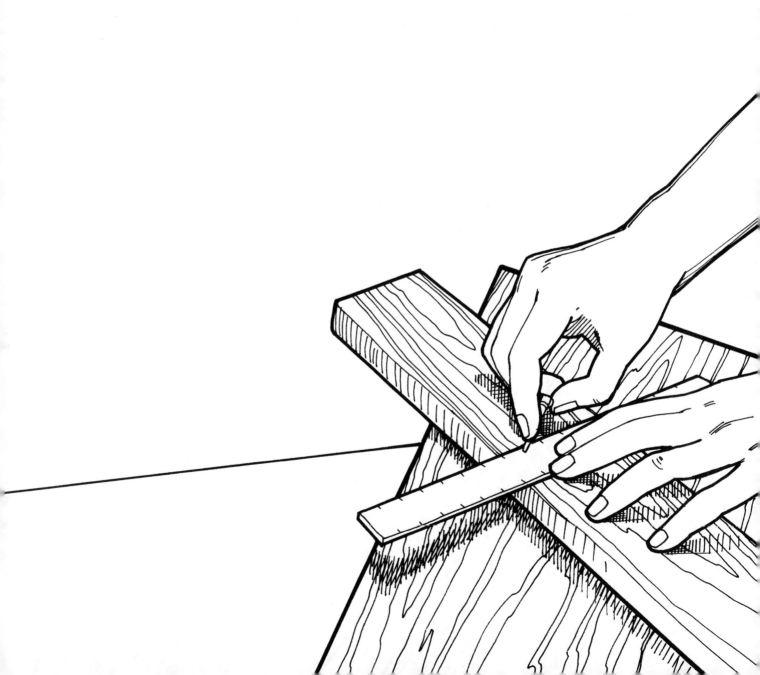

CARTOONIST

SATIRE

Comics are an important forum in popular culture. They can be a humorous reflection of our lives or a means of social commentary.

HUMOR

BOOKS

This field is a great idea for a storybook that hasn't been written yet!

Illustrations by Sally Schaedler © Susan Striker

COMPUTER ARTIST

Computers are one of the newest tools
artists use to express themselves.

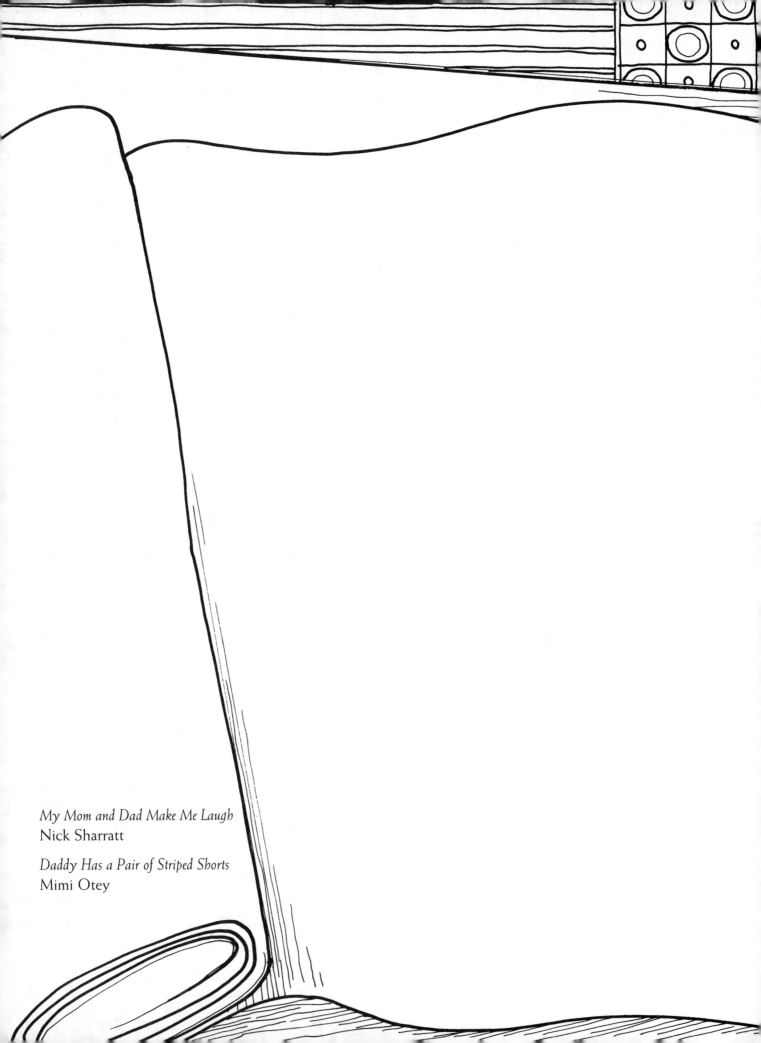

My Mom and Dad Make Me Laugh
Nick Sharratt

Daddy Has a Pair of Striped Shorts
Mimi Otey

FABRIC DESIGNER

Fabric designers decorate material to be worn as clothing or used in interiors. This bolt of fabric will have your distinctive design on it.

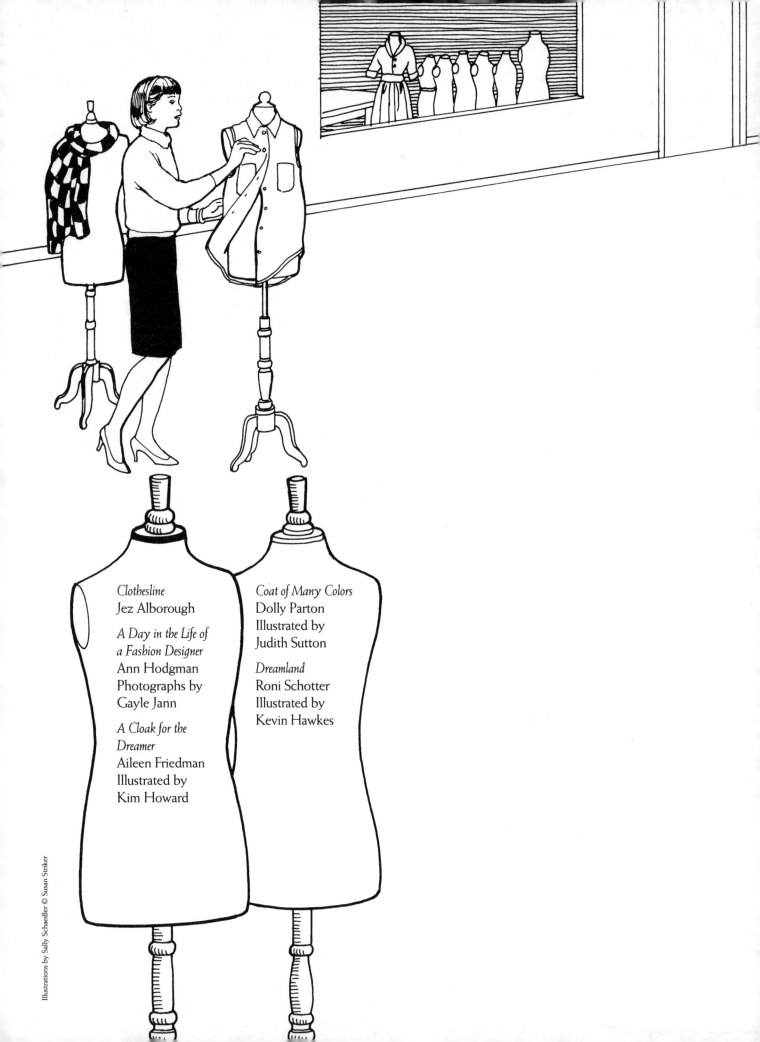

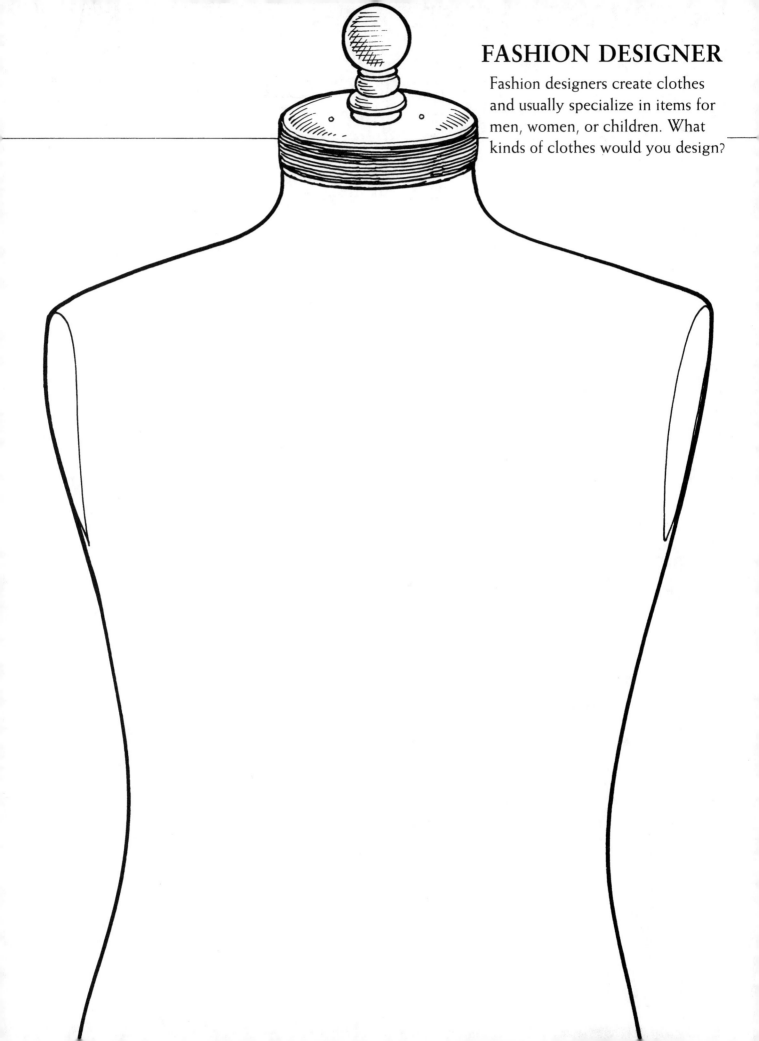

FASHION DESIGNER

Fashion designers create clothes and usually specialize in items for men, women, or children. What kinds of clothes would you design?

Ida Makes a
Movie
Kay Chorao

Flicks
Tomie de Paola

Lights! Camera! Action!
Gail Gibbons

Filmmakers create their own art on celluloid.

Furniture designers must take beauty and comfort into consideration when they design furniture for the home and office.

A Chair for My Mother
Vera B. Williams

Peter's Chair
Ezra Jack Keats

Graphic designers are responsible for designing visual images that reflect a business or product.

GRAPHIC DESIGNER
We design logos

The Whispering Cloth:
A Refugee's Story
Pegi Deitz Shea
Illustrated by Anita Riggio
Stitched by You Yang

Life Around the Lake
Maricel E. Presilla and Gloria S

Magical Hands, Marjorie Barker

Gittel's Hands, Erica Silverman
Illustrated by Deborah Nourse
Lattimore

My Hands Can, Jean Holzenthaler
Illustrated by Nancy Tafuri

Daisy and Her Needles
Keith Balding

Mola: Cuna Life Stories and Art
Maricel E. Presilla

HANDICRAFT ARTIST Craftspersons can use their hands for stitchery, needlepoint, or quilting.

INDUSTRIAL DESIGNER

Industrial designers are responsible for the aesthetic appeal of products such as typewriters, copy machines, automobiles, calculators, computers, and telephones. What would this work area look like if you became an industrial designer?

JEWELRY
DESIGNER

A jewelry designer creates
earrings, pins, necklaces,
and rings and may even be
commissioned to create a
new crown for royalty.

Earrings
Judith Viorst, Illustrated by
Nola Langner Malone

The Bracelet
Yoshiko Uchida
Illustrated by Joanna Yardey

Grandma's Jewelry Box
Linda Milstein
Illustrated by Jean Hirashima

Illustrations by Sally Schaedler © Susan Striker

Sunflower House
Eve Bunting, Illustrated by
Kathryn Hewitt

Miss Rumphius
Barbara Cooney

Grandma's Garden
Elaine Moore
Illustrated by Dan Andersen

Flower Garden
Eve Bunting, Illustrated by
Kathryn Hewitt

LANDSCAPE
ARCHITECTS

Landscape architects
use plants and trees to
beautify the environment.

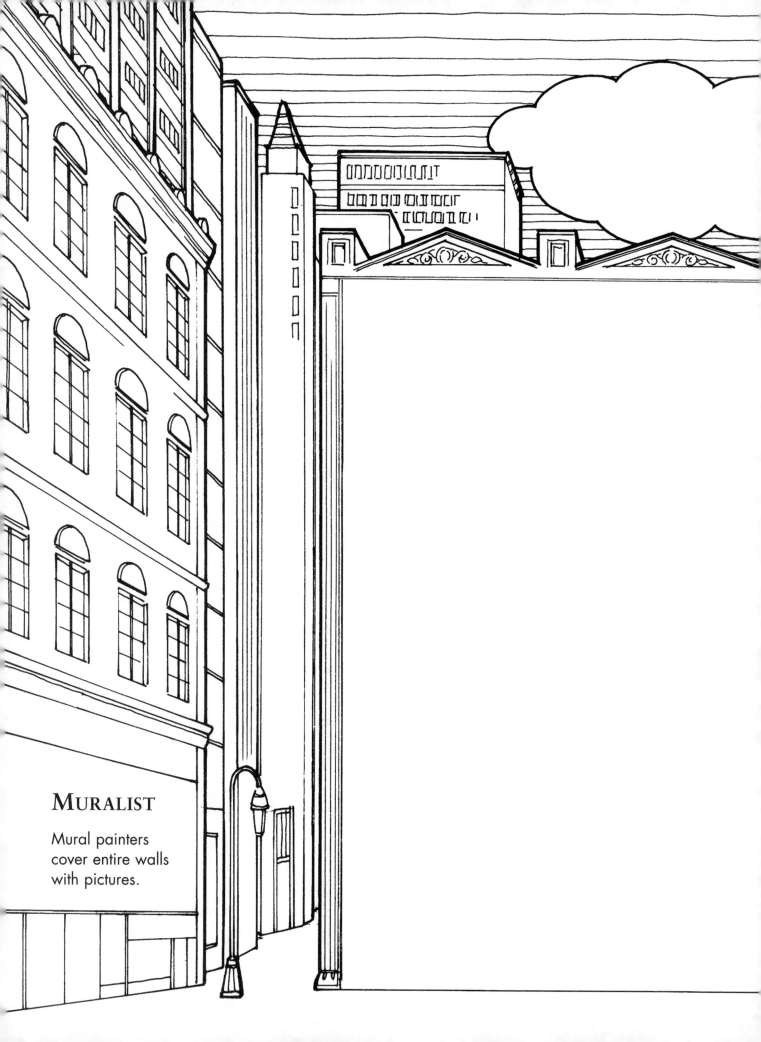

MURALIST

Mural painters
cover entire walls
with pictures.

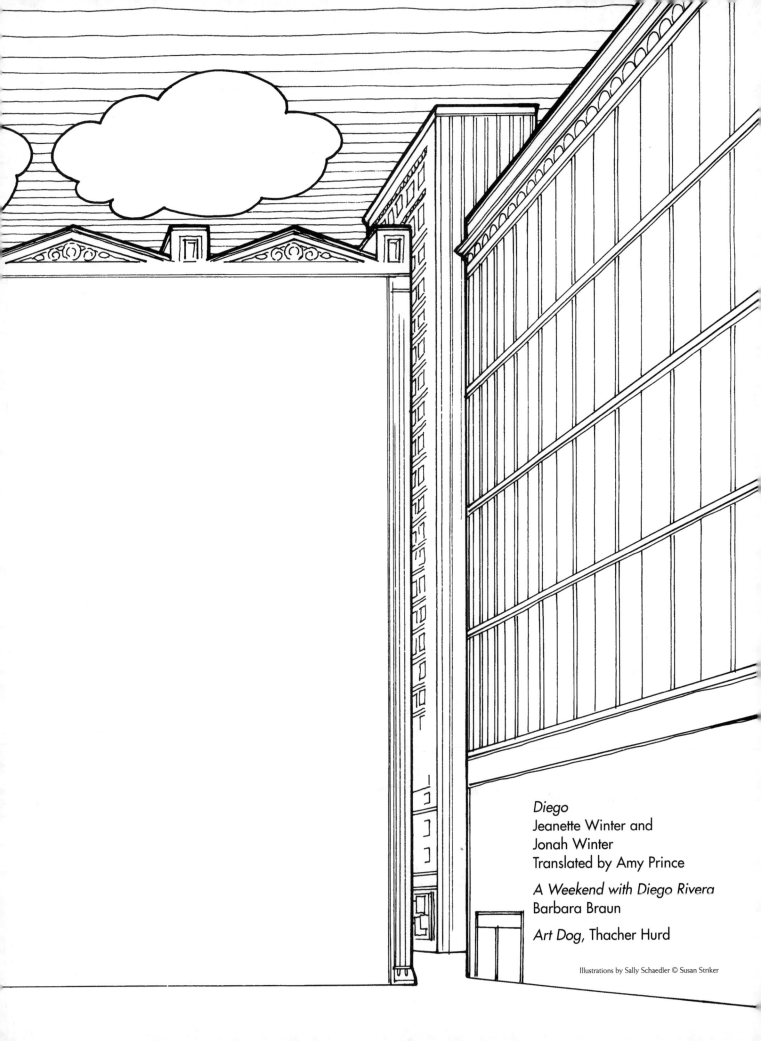

Diego
Jeanette Winter and
Jonah Winter
Translated by Amy Prince

A Weekend with Diego Rivera
Barbara Braun

Art Dog, Thacher Hurd

Illustrations by Sally Schaedler © Susan Striker

MUSEUM/ GALLERY CURATOR

A museum curator collects and displays art for museums. What works of art would you put in this museum?

A Tale of Two Williams
Diana Golden and Inge Heckel
Photographs by Carl Mydans

The Gentleman and the Kitchen Maid
Diane Stanley
Illustrated by Dennis Nolan

A Visit to the Art Galaxy
Annie Reiner

A Visit to the Sesame Street Museum
Children's Television Workshop

Visiting the Art Museum
Laurene Krasny and Mark Brown

Max the Art Lover
Neugebauer Press USA

Ella's Trip to the Museum
Elaine Clayton

Jamaica Louise James
Amy Hest
Illustrated by Sheila White Santon

The Witches' Supermarket
Susan Meddaugh

McGraw's Emporium
Jim Aylesworth
Illustrated by Mavis Smith

Illustrations by Sally Schaedler © ᶜ

PACKAGE
DESIGNER

You have been asked to create
packaging for a new line of food.

POTTER

The Magic Vase, Fiona French
The Little Lump of Clay, Diana Engel

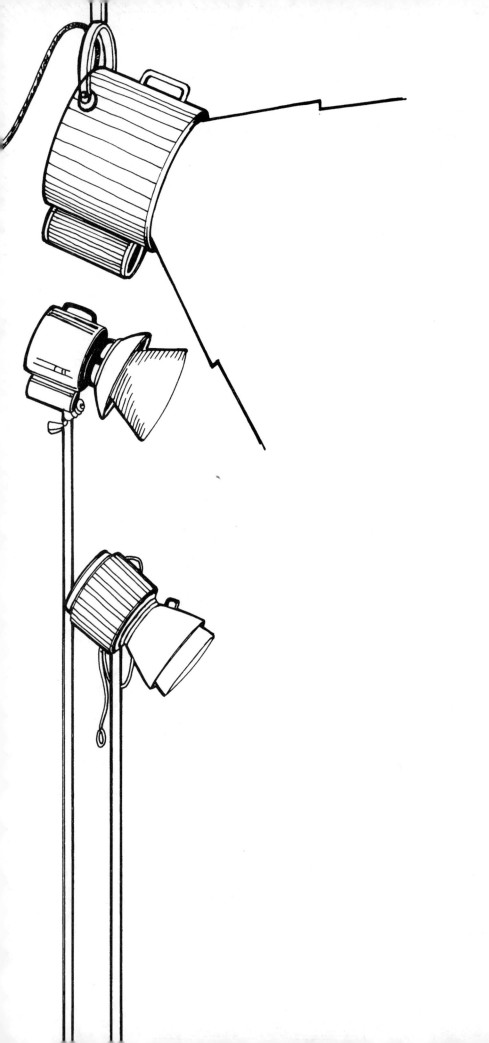

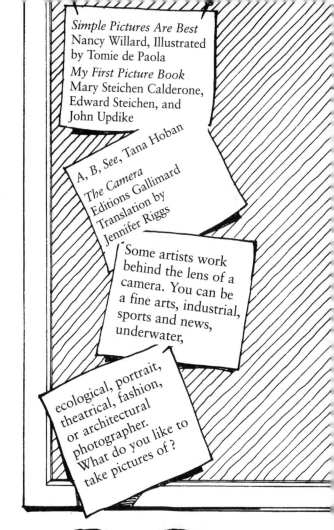

Simple Pictures Are Best
Nancy Willard, Illustrated by Tomie de Paola

My First Picture Book
Mary Steichen Calderone, Edward Steichen, and John Updike

A, B, See, Tana Hoban

The Camera Editions Gallimard Translation by Jennifer Riggs

Some artists work behind the lens of a camera. You can be a fine arts, industrial, sports and news, underwater, ecological, portrait, theatrical, fashion, or architectural photographer. What do you like to take pictures of?

PHOTOGRAPHER

POLICE ARTIST

Police artists create portraits of criminals based on descriptions given by witnesses and victims.

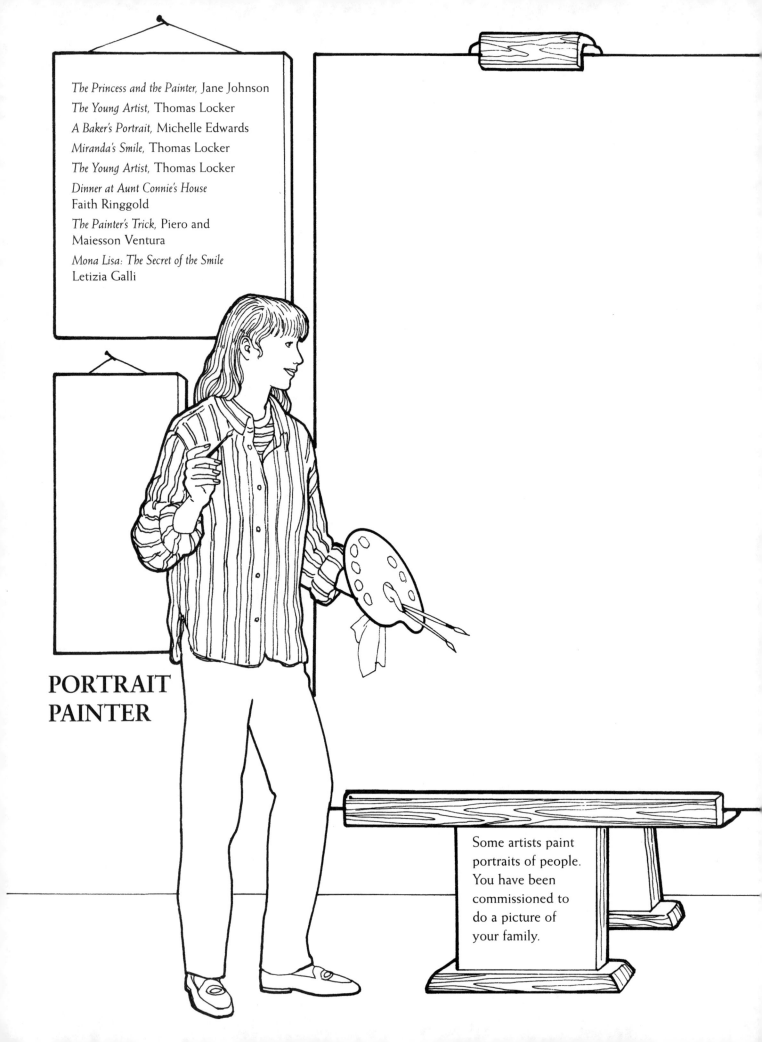

PORTRAIT
PAINTER

Some artists paint
portraits of people.
You have been
commissioned to
do a picture of
your family.

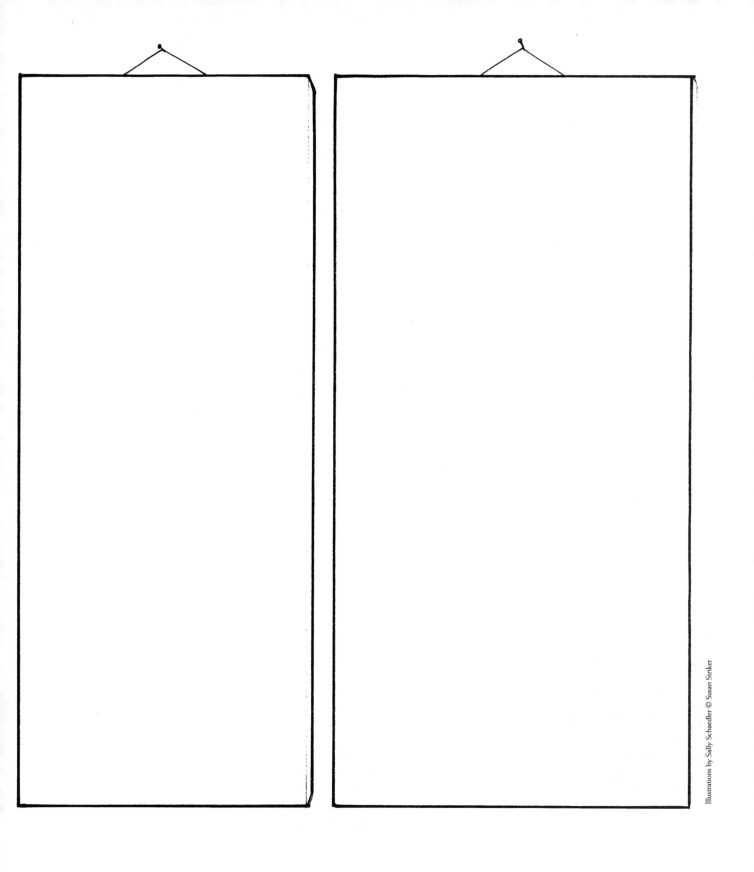

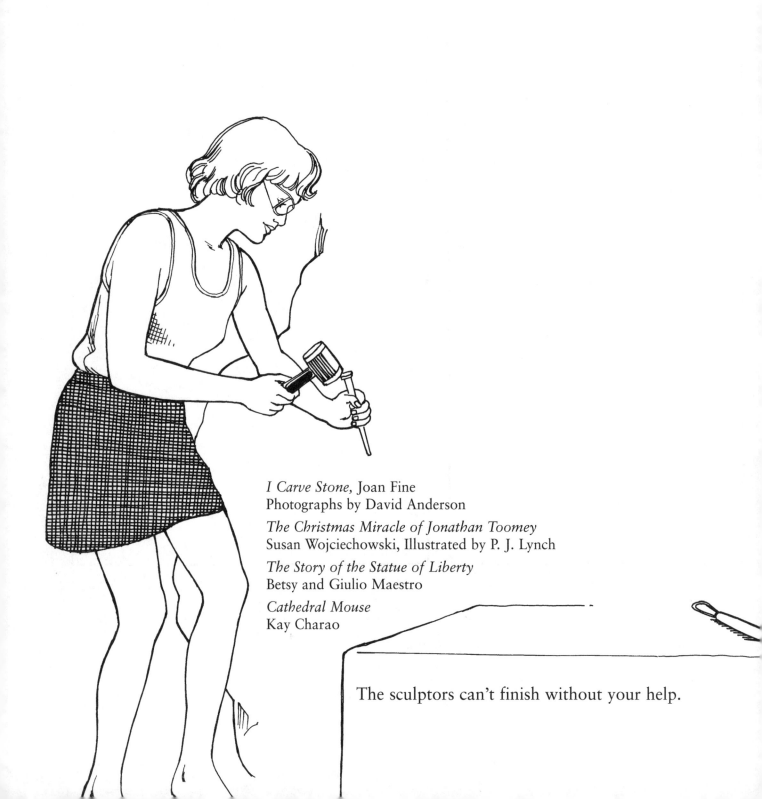

The sculptors can't finish without your help.

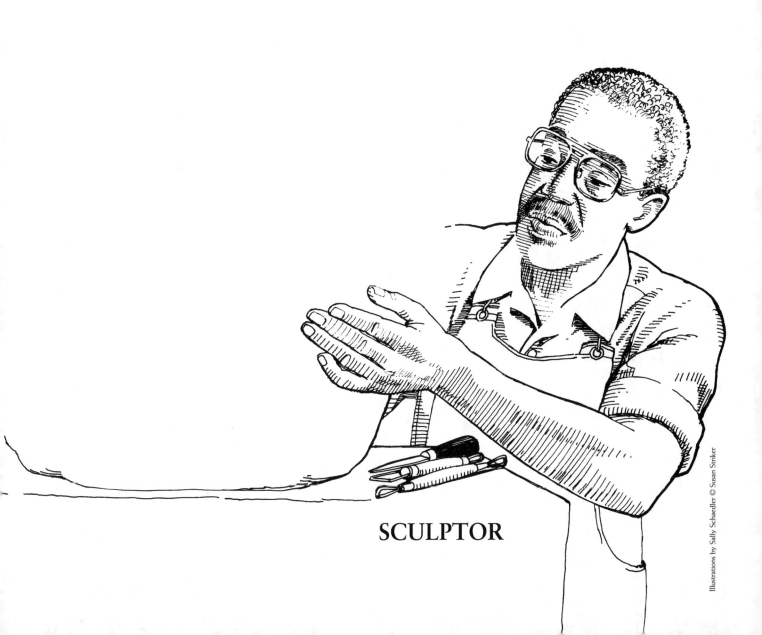

SCULPTOR

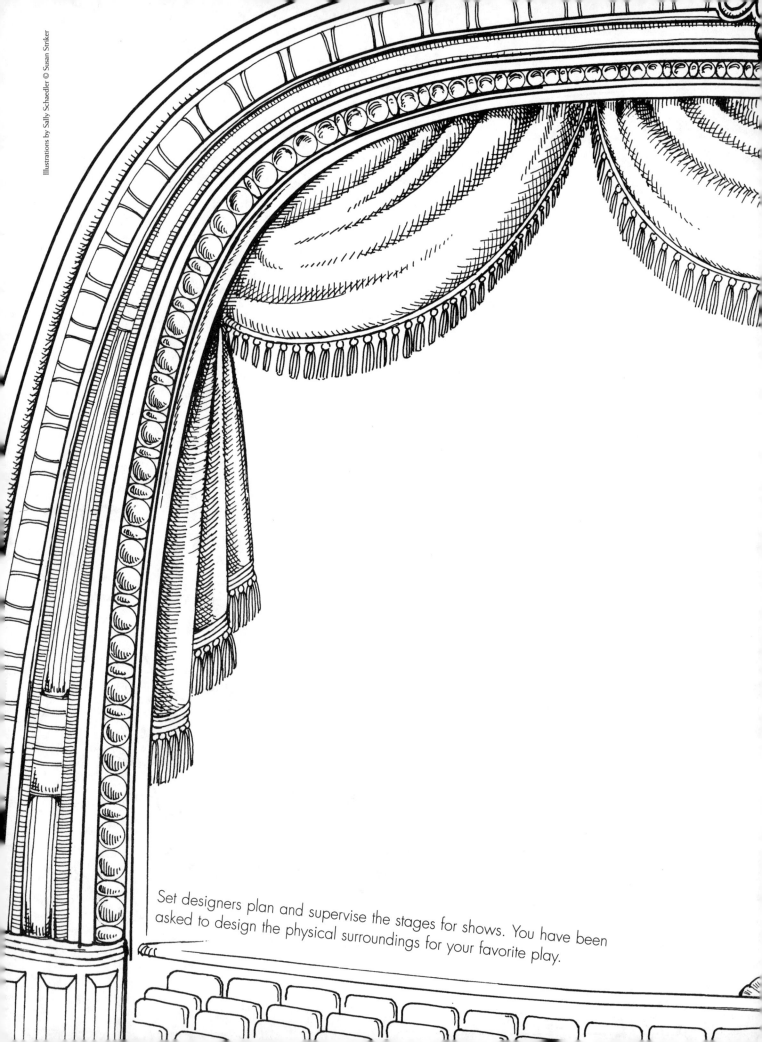

Set designers plan and supervise the stages for shows. You have been asked to design the physical surroundings for your favorite play.

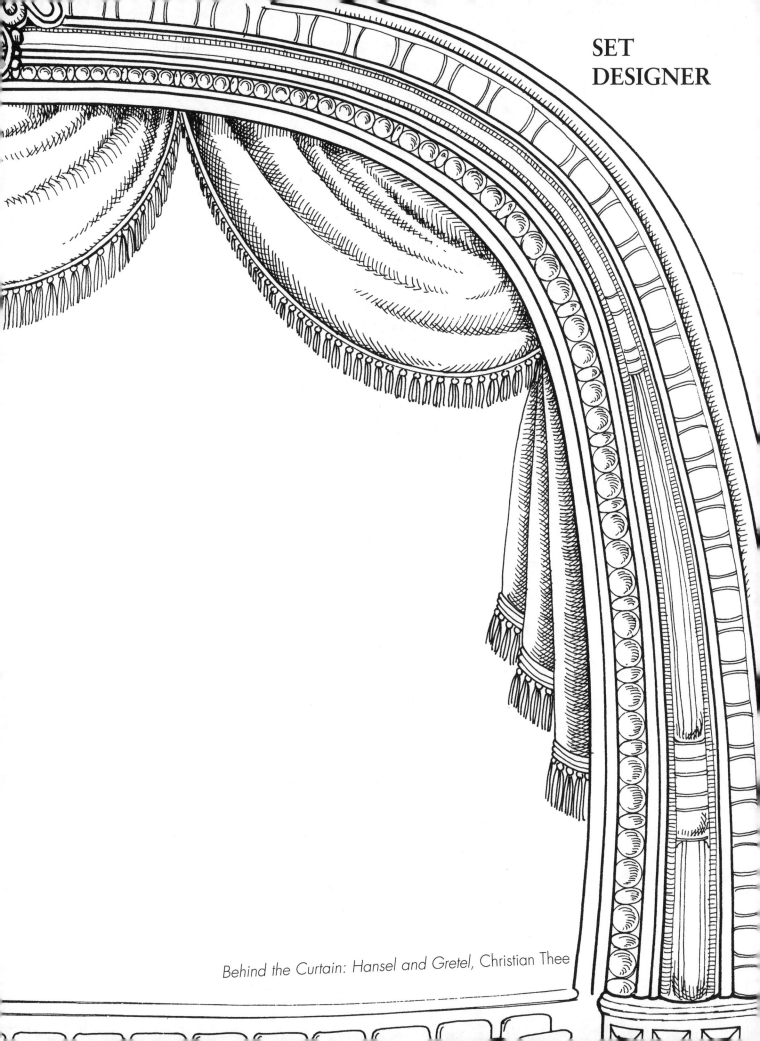

Behind the Curtain: Hansel and Gretel, Christian Thee

The Anti-Coloring Book® by Susan Striker and Edward Kimmel
General interest, for ages 6 and older.
ISBN 0-8050-0246-4

The Second Anti-Coloring Book® by Susan Striker with Edward Kimmel
General interest, for ages 6 and older.
ISBN 0-8050-0771-7

The Third Anti-Coloring Book® by Susan Striker
General interest, for ages 6 and older.
ISBN 0-8050-1447-0

The Fourth Anti-Coloring Book® by Susan Striker
General interest, for ages 6 and older.
ISBN 0-8050-2000-4

The Fifth Anti-Coloring Book® by Susan Striker
General interest, for ages 6 and older.
ISBN 0-8050-2376-3

The Sixth Anti-Coloring Book® by Susan Striker
General interest, for ages 6 and older.
ISBN 0-8050-0873-X

The Anti-Coloring Book® **of Exploring Space on Earth** by Susan Striker
Architecture and interior design.
ISBN 0-8050-1446-2

The Anti-Coloring Book® **of Masterpieces** by Susan Striker
The world's great art, including color reproductions.
ISBN 0-8050-2644-4

The Inventor's Anti-Coloring Book® by Susan Striker
Inventions, devices, and contraptions.
ISBN 0-8050-2615-0

The Mystery Anti-Coloring Book® by Susan Striker
Mysteries, discoveries, and cops and robbers.
ISBN 0-8050-1600-7

The Newspaper Anti-Coloring Book® by Susan Striker
Write and illustrate your own newspaper.
ISBN 0-8050-1599-X

The Circus Anti-Coloring Book® by Susan Striker with Jason Striker
Clowns, acrobats, and everything else under the big top.
ISBN 0-8050-3412-9

The Anti-Coloring Book ® **of Celebrations** by Susan Striker
Literature-based activities for holidays from around the world.
ISBN 0-8050-3414-5

Artists at Work by Susan Striker
A literature-based Anti-Coloring Book® on careers in art.
ISBN 0-8050-3413-7

Look for these at your local bookstore.